LAUGH TWICE AND CALL ME IN THE MORNING

Selected by
BRUCE LANSKY

mMeadowbrook Press
Distributed by Simon & Schuster
New York

Library of Congress Cataloging-in-Publication Data
Laugh twice and call me in the morning / selected by Bruce Lansky.
    p.   cm.
   ISBN 0-88166-326-3 (Meadowbrook).—ISBN 0-671-31656-7 (Simon & Schuster)
   1. Health—Humor. 2. American wit and humor. I. Lansky, Bruce.
   PN6231.H38L38   1998
   610'.2'07—dc21   98-53471
                                                         CIP

Editor: Bruce Lansky
Coordinating Editor: Heather Hooper
Production Manager: Joe Gagne
Production Assistant: Danielle White
Cover Art: Jack Lindstrom

NOTICE: Every effort has been made to locate the copyright owners of the material used in this book. Please let us know of any errors, and we will gladly make any necessary corrections in subsequent printings.

Published by Meadowbrook Press, 5451 Smetana Drive, Minnetonka, Minnesota 55343

www.meadowbrookpress.com

BOOK TRADE DISTRIBUTION by Simon & Schuster, a division of Simon and Schuster, Inc., 1230 Avenue of the Americas, New York, NY 10020

02 01 00 99   10 9 8 7 6 5 4 3 2

Printed in the United States of America

CONTENTS

ACKNOWLEDGMENTS

We would like to thank the individuals
who served on a reading panel for this project:

Polly Andersen, David W. Arbogast, Ann Ballard, Michael N. Ballard, Ken Bastien, Gail Clark, Jennifer De Boef, Jennifer Dillard, Dorothy Francis, Mary Beth Gradziel, Maxine Hartman, Sydnie Meltzer Kleinhenz, Cynthia MacGregor, Charlene Meltzer, Lois Muehl, Steve Roe, Heidi Roemer, Cindy Schielke, Rita Schlachter, Rosemary Schmidt, Brad Schreiber, Diane Z. Shore, Denise Ann Tiffany, Timothy Tocher, Esther Towns, Debra Tracy, Toni Webb, Dina Wren

INTRODUCTION

They say that laughter is the best medicine. Norman Cousins wrote *Anatomy of an Illness as Perceived by the Patient*, a book that documented his amazing success in treating a crippling and supposedly irreversible disease with, among other things, Marx Brothers' movies.

If the Marx Brothers can help Norman Cousins, then imagine the therapeutic benefit of reading a collection of the funniest things ever said or written about health by Erma Bombeck, Lily Tomlin, Roy Blount, Jr., Ellen DeGeneres, Conan O'Brian, Rodney Dangerfield, Mark Twain, and others. You might never have to visit a doctor, dentist, or therapist again.

Keep in mind, though, that four out of five doctors recommend reading this book *before* you make an appointment with them. The reason is simple: If you read *Laugh Twice and Call Me in the Morning* in the doctor's waiting room, chances are very high that by the time the nurse summons you to the doctor's office, the pain that had brought you will be gone. Without a trace. And you won't be able to remember why you made the appointment in the first place. So read this book at the first sign of discomfort. You'll be glad you did. And so will your HMO.

Bruce Lansky

A SHORT HISTORY OF MEDICINE:
"Doctor, I have an earache."

2000 B.C. "Here, eat this root."
1000 B.C. "That root is heathen,
say this prayer."
1850 A.D. "That prayer is superstition,
drink this potion."
1940 A.D. "That potion is snake oil,
swallow this pill."
1985 A.D. "That pill is ineffective,
take this antibiotic."
2000 A.D. "That antibiotic is artificial.
Here, eat this root!"

—Anonymous

Never go to a doctor whose
office plants have died.
—*Erma Bombeck*

The art of medicine consists of amusing the
patient while Nature cures the disease.
—*Voltaire*

I recently became a Christian Scientist. It was
the only health plan I could afford.
—*Betsy Salkind*

Fact: 50 percent of the doctors practicing in this country today graduated in the lower half of their class.
—*Ron Dentinger*

Doctors and lawyers must go to school for years and years, often with little sleep and with great sacrifice to their first wives.
—*Roy Blount, Jr.*

A doctor and a lawyer were talking at a party.

"You know, Barry," said the doctor, "I hate it when people come up to me at a party to tell me what's wrong with them. They expect me to dish out free advice right on the spot. Does that ever happen to you?"

"All the time," assured the lawyer.

"What do you do?"

"Well, the next morning I send them a bill that reads 'Fees incurred at party last night—$25.' That soon stops it."

"That's a good idea. I'll try it!"

The next morning the doctor received a letter from the lawyer that read, "Fees incurred at party last night—$25."

—Anonymous

"We medical practitioners do our very best, Mr. Nyman. Nothing is more sacred to us than the doctor-plaintiff relationship."

"I hope you're not going to be like the twenty incompetent doctors who couldn't find anything wrong with me."

Hypochondria is the only disease
hypochondriacs don't think they have.
—*Fred Metcalf*

Hypochondriac: Someone who feels bad
when he feels good because he knows
he'll feel worse when he feels better.
—*Anonymous*

Epitaph for a hypochondriac:
I told you so!
—*Anonymous*

My sister's asthmatic and in the middle of an attack she got an obscene phone call. The guy on the other end of the line said, "Did I call you or did you call me?"
—*John Mendoza*

It must be February. My nose runs and my car doesn't.
—*Ron Dentinger*

This woman sneezed like 300 times. She said, "There must be something in the air." I said, "Yeah, your germs."
—*Linda Herskovic*

Patient: When I touch my tongue to aluminum foil wrapped around a walnut while holding a toaster oven, I feel a peculiar tingling in my toes. . . . What's wrong with me, doctor?

Doctor: You have too much spare time.

—*Dan Piraro*

"Doctor, Doctor, you've got to help me! I just can't stop my hands from shaking!"

"Do you drink a lot?"

"Not really. I spill most of it!"

—*Anonymous*

A fellow walked into a doctor's office and the receptionist asked him what he had.

He said, "Shingles."

So she took down his name, address, and medical insurance number and told him to have a seat.

A few minutes later a nurse's aid came out and asked him what he had.

He said, "Shingles."

So she took down his height, weight, and a complete medical history and told him to wait in the examining room.

Ten minutes later a nurse came in and asked him what he had.

He said, "Shingles."

So she gave him a blood test, a blood pressure test, and an electrocardiogram and told him to take off all his clothes and wait for the doctor.

Fifteen minutes later the doctor came in and asked him what he had.

He said, "Shingles."

The doctor said, "Where?"

He said, "Outside in the truck. Where do you want them?"

—Anonymous

A man walks into a doctor's office. He has a cucumber up his nose, a carrot in his left ear, and a banana in his right ear.

"What's the matter with me?" he asks the doctor.

The doctor replies, "You're not eating properly."
—*Anonymous*

A man with a worried look on his face ran into a clinic and asked the doctor if he knew a way to stop the hiccups. Without any warning, the doctor slapped him in the face. Amazed and angry, the young man demanded that the doctor explain his unusual behavior.

"Well," said the doctor, "you don't have the hiccups now, do you?"

"No," answered the young man, "but my wife out in the car still does!"
—*Anonymous*

A ninety-year-old man went to his doctor and said, "Doctor, my wife—who is eighteen—is expecting a baby."

The doctor said, "Let me tell you a story. A man went hunting, but instead of his gun, he picked up an umbrella by mistake. And when a bear suddenly charged at him, he pointed his umbrella at the bear, shot, and killed it on the spot."

"Impossible. Somebody else must have shot that bear."

"Exactly my point."

—*Anonymous*

A **doctor** and his wife were having a big argument at breakfast.

"You aren't so good in bed either!" he shouted and stormed off to work.

By **midmorning**, the doctor decided he'd better make amends and so he phoned home. After many rings, his wife picked up the phone.

"What took you so long to answer?"

"I was in bed."

"What were you doing in bed this late?"

"Getting a second opinion."

—Anonymous

A while back, my neighbor was telling me that his entire body hurt. To demonstrate he took his finger and began to press on various parts of his body. He poked his ribs and said, "This hurts."

He pressed his arm and said, "Ouch! That hurts too."

He pressed his foot and said, "It even hurts if I press down here on my foot."

I told him to see a doctor. He did. Turns out he had a broken finger.

—*Ron Dentinger*

Patient: Doc, every time I drink coffee, I get a stabbing sensation in my eye.

Doctor: Next time, take the spoon out of the cup.

—*Anonymous*

Sherman gets a call from his doctor with the results of his blood test.

"I've got bad news and worse news," says the doctor. "The bad news is that you've only got twenty-four hours to live."

"Oh, no," says Sherman. "That's terrible. How can it get any worse than that?"

"I've been trying to reach you since yesterday."
—*Anonymous*

My doctor likes to break things to me gently. The other day I asked her, "Doc, is it serious?" She said, "Only if you have plans for next year!"
—*Anonymous*

"This, Mr. Carlisle, is what we found lodged in your skull."

A woman accompanied her husband to the doctor's office. After the checkup, the doctor took the wife aside and told her, "If you don't do the following, your husband will surely die:

- "Each morning, fix him a healthy breakfast and send him off to work in a good mood.

- "For dinner, fix his favorite meal, and don't burden him with household chores.

- "Finally, have sex with him every night."

On the way home, the husband asked the wife what the doctor had said to her. She said, "You're going to die."

—*Anonymous*

A doctor was doing his daily rounds in the hospital when a nurse noticed he had a rectal thermometer tucked behind his ear. The nurse approached the doctor and whispered into his ear, "Doctor, doctor, you have a rectal thermometer behind your ear."

The doctor took the rectal thermometer out from behind his ear and stated in disgust, "Some asshole must have my pen!"

—Anonymous

The doctor didn't stay long with the patient. As she left the house, she told the patient's wife, "There's nothing wrong with your husband. He just thinks he's sick."

After a few days the doctor called to see if her diagnosis had been correct. "How's your husband?" she asked.

"He's worse," said the wife. "Now he thinks he's dead."

—Anonymous

ACTUAL DOCTORS' NAMES:

Dr. Barker, Veterinarian

Dr. Hacker, Surgeon

Dr. Skinner, Dermatologist

Dr. Born, Ob-gyn

Dr. Groth, Oncologist

Dr. Dick, Urologist

Dr. Butt, Gastroenterology

Dr. Tickles, Pediatrician

Dr. Looney, Psychiatrist

Dr. Vu, Radiologist

Dr. Bone, Orthopedics

Dr. Gore, Emergency Medicine

Dr. Kidd, Pediatrician

Dr. Strange, Mental Health Director

Dr. Foote, Podiatrist

—*Anonymous*

Specialist: A man who knows more and more about less and less.
—*William J. Mayo*

Specialist: A doctor who has a smaller practice, but a larger house.
—*Ron Dentinger*

In this era of specialization, what four out of five doctors end up recommending is another doctor.
—*Jeff Rovin*

Pediatricians are men of little patients.
—*Shelby Friedman*

There are only two things a child will share willingly—communicable diseases and his mother's age.
—*Benjamin Spock*

Insanity is hereditary. You can get it from your children.
—*Sam Levenson*

These are actual excuse notes from parents:

#1. My son is under a doctor's care and should not take PE today. Please execute him.

#2. Please excuse Lisa for being absent. She was sick and I had her shot.

#3. Dear school: Please ekscuse John being absent on January 28, 29, 30, 31, 32, and 33.

#4. Please excuse Tommy for being absent yesterday. He had diarrhea and his boots leak.

#5. Please excuse Mary for being absent yesterday. She was in bed with gramps.
—*Nisheeth Parekh, University of Texas Medical Branch in Galveston*

DISTANCE LENDS SOMETHING OR OTHER

I don't wear glasses, but I place
The print some distance from my face;
A distance that increases yearly
If I would read the letter clearly.

I don't wear glasses, though I fear
I'll have to, almost any year.
My eyes, I find, are plenty strong enough;
It's only that my arms aren't long enough.

—Richard Armour

A certain eye specialist is supposed to have successfully treated the great surrealist painter Salvador Dali. For his fee, the specialist requested that Dali paint something for him, on a subject of Dali's own choosing.

The grateful Dali therefore painted an enormous eye in meticulous detail and in its very pupil, he placed a small but perfect portrait of the doctor.

The ophthalmologist looked at the painting with awe and astonishment and said, "Well, Mr. Dali, I can only say that I am glad I'm not a proctologist."

—Isaac Asimov

If you don't see what you want,
you've come to the right place.
—*Sign in optometrist's window*

If carrots are so good for the eyes, how come I
see so many dead rabbits on the highway?
—*Richard Jeni*

"I've been seeing spots in front of my eyes."

"Have you seen a doctor?"

"No, just spots."

—*Anonymous*

Doctor: Mrs. Larson, you're not going deaf in your left ear—you seem to have a suppository stuck in there.

Mrs. Larson: Well, now I know what happened to my hearing aid.

—*Anonymous*

I went to the doctor to get rid of the annoying ringing in my ears. The ringing is gone. Now I've got a dial tone.

—*Ron Dentinger*

A male gynecologist is like an auto mechanic who has never owned a car.
—*Carrie Snow*

I got a postcard from my gynecologist. It said, "Did you know it's time for your checkup?" No, but now my mailman does.
—*Cathy Ladman*

"I am very concerned," Lori said to the doctor. "Ever since you told me to use a diaphragm, I've been urinating purple."

"That's very unusual," said the doctor. "What kind of jelly are you using?"

"Grape."

—*Anonymous*

After several years as an ob-gyn, a doctor decides he's tired of what he's been doing and wants to change his career. He wonders what other types of work he can do. After a while, the ob-gyn remembers how much he liked automotive class in school and since he's good with his hands, he decides to become an auto mechanic. He enrolls at the community college automotive school. Upon his completion of the course, the final exam consists of taking a car engine apart and put-ting it back together. The doctor turns in his final project and, to his astonishment, receives a grade of 150 percent. After class, the ob-gyn says to the instructor, "You know, I've gotten plenty of 100 percents in my life, but how does someone get a 150 percent?

"Well," responds the instructor, "I gave you 50 percent for taking the engine apart, 50 percent for putting the engine back together, and another 50percent for doing everything through the muffler!"

—*Anonymous*

A man speaks frantically into the phone. "My wife is pregnant, and her contractions are only two minutes apart!"

"Is this her first child?" the doctor queries.

"No, you *idiot!*" the man shouts. "This is her husband!"
—*Anonymous*

Ole and Lena went to the hospital so Lena could give birth to their first baby. As Ole waited in the lobby, the doctor came out to inform him that he had some good news and some bad news. "The good news is that you have a normal baby boy. The bad news is that it is a cesarean."

Ole started crying: "Vel, I'm glad it is a healthy baby . . . but I vas kinda hoping it vould be a Norwegian."
—*Red Stangland*

An elderly woman went into the doctor's office. When the doctor asked why she was there, she replied, "I'd like to have some birth control pills."

Taken aback, the doctor thought for a minute and then said, "Excuse me, Mrs. Smith, but you're seventy-five years old. What possible use could you have for birth control pills?"

The woman responded, "They help me sleep better."

The doctor thought some more and continued, "How in the world do birth control pills help you to sleep?"

The woman said, "I put them in my granddaughter's orange juice and I sleep better at night."

—*Anonymous*

A man was running late for an appointment with a urologist. When he got to the medical center, he inadvertently walked into the podiatry department that is located next to urology.

"Sorry I'm late," he said to the nurse.

"I can't seem to find your chart, Mr. Jones," she said. "Why don't you have a seat in the treatment room and the doctor will be right with you." The patient took a seat and after a while the podiatrist entered the room.

"Let's have a look," the doctor said. Mr. Jones stood up and unzipped his trousers and proceeded to show the doctor his problem. "That's not a foot!!!" the podiatrist exclaimed.

"I didn't know there was a minimum requirement," replied the patient.

—*Anonymous*

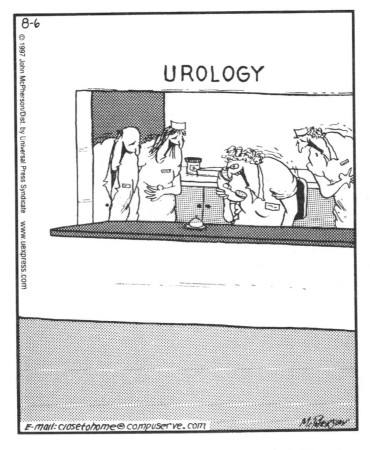

"Urology department. Can you hold?"

THINGS YOU DON'T WANT TO HEAR
DURING SURGERY:

Oops!

Come back with that! Bad dog!

Hand me that . . . uh . . . that uh . . . thingie.

Damn, there go the lights again.

Ya know, there's big money in kidneys. Hell, this guy's got two of 'em.

Everybody stand back! I lost my contact lens!

What do you mean he wasn't in for a sex change?

I hope this patient already has some kids.

Nurse, did this patient sign the organ donation card?

Better save that. We'll need it for the autopsy.

—*Anonymous*

I was going to have cosmetic surgery until I noticed that the doctor's office was full of portraits by Picasso.
—*Rita Rudner*

You know it's time for a second opinion when your neurosurgeon calls your case a "no-brainer."
—*W. Asbury Stembridge, Jr.*

Patient: Nurse, during my operation I heard the surgeon use a four-letter word that upset me very much.

Nurse: What word was that?

Patient: Oops!
—*Anonymous*

All them surgeons—they're highway robbers.
Why do you think they wear masks
when they work on you?
—*Archie Bunker*

They can take the fat from your rear and
use it to bang out the dents in your face.
Now, that's what I call recycling. It gives a
whole new meaning to dancing
cheek to cheek.
—*Anita Wise*

She got her good looks from her father.
He's a plastic surgeon.
—*Groucho Marx*

Doctor: If I find the operation necessary, would you have the money to pay for it?

Patient: If I didn't have the money, would you find the operation necessary?
—*Fred Metcalf*

Our doctor would never really operate unless it was necessary. He was just that way.
If he didn't need the money, he wouldn't lay a hand on you.
—*Herb Shriner*

I wonder why ye can always read a doctor's bill an' ye niver can read his purscription.
—*Finley Peter Dunne*

A fashionable surgeon, like a pelican, can be recognized by the size of his bill.
—*J. Chalmers Da Costa*

I got the bill for my surgery. Now I know what the doctors were wearing those masks for.
—*James H. Boren*

I can't figure out what covers less—
the hospital gown or my insurance company.
—*Gene Perret*

A hospital should also have a recovery room
adjoining the cashier's office.
—*Francis O'Walsh*

If you've got your health, you've got everything.
And if you don't have your health, sooner or
later your doctor has everything.
—*Gene Perret*

Doctor: I can't do anything about your condition. I'm afraid it's hereditary.

Patient: In that case, send the bill to my parents.

—*Joe Claro*

My grandfather always used to ask me, "What's more important, your money or your health?"

I'd say, "My health."

He'd say, "Great, can you lend me twenty bucks?"

—*Anonymous*

"Of course you're furious over the price of your medication, Mrs. Grimwald—that's one of its side effects."

I once asked my doctor, "How can I ever repay your kindness?"

He said, "Check or cash."
                    —*Milton Berle*

The doctor's nurse called a patient: "Your check came back."

The patient said, "So did my arthritis!"
                    —*Milton Berle*

Doctor: Did you recover from your operation?

Patient: No, I still have three more payments.
                    —*Milton Berle*

The instructions read, "Take one pill, three times a day." How am I supposed to do that? Tie a string to it?

—*Anonymous*

Patient: I told the pharmacist about my symptoms.

Doctor: What sort of foolish advice did he give you?

Patient: He told me to see you.

—*Ron Dentinger*

I called my acupuncturist and told him I was in terrible pain. He told me to take two safety pins and call him in the morning.

—*Fred Metcalf*

Did you hear about the three men who hijacked a truck full of Viagra? The police are looking for a gang of hardened criminals.

—*Anonymous*

Q: How is Viagra like Disneyland?

A: You have to wait an hour for a three-minute ride.

—*Anonymous*

The price of Prozac went up 50 percent last year. When they asked Prozac users how they felt about this, they said "Whatever. . . ."

—*Conan O'Brien*

After giving a woman a complete medical examination, the doctor explained his prescription. "Take the green pill with a glass of water when you wake up. Take the blue pill with a glass of water after lunch. Then just before going to bed, take the red pill with a glass of water."

"Exactly what is my problem, Doctor?" the woman asked.

"You're not drinking enough water."
—*Anonymous*

The doctor handed her overweight patient a bottle of pills. "Don't take these pills," she said. "Spill them on the floor and pick them up one by one."
—*Joe Claro*

I saw a commercial on TV the other day for Preparation H that said, "Kiss your hemorrhoids good-bye." Not even if I could.
—*John Mendoza*

I tried Flintstones vitamins. I didn't feel any better, but I could stop the car with my feet.
—*Joan St. Onge*

What's great about aspirin is that no matter how long you suck on it, it never loses its flavor.
—*Gregg Rogell*

"I came to make an appointment with the dentist," said the man to the receptionist.

"I'm sorry, sir," she replied. "He's out right now, but. . . ."

"Thank you," interrupted the obviously nervous patient. "When will he be out again?"

—Anonymous

When a dentist says, "This may sting a little," he really means, "How high can you jump?"
—Lewis Grizzard

My dentist said, "This might hurt a little." Then he pulled out my wisdom tooth.

I told my dentist, "This might hurt a little." Then I pulled out my empty wallet.

—Bruce Lansky

"For goodness sakes!" cried a dentist as he examined a new patient. "You have the biggest cavity I've ever seen! The biggest cavity I've ever seen!"

"You didn't have to repeat yourself," the patient grumbled.

"I didn't," the dentist replied. "That was an echo."
—*Michael J. Pellowski*

I finally have a dental plan. I chew
on the other side.
—*Janine DiTullio*

Be true to your teeth or your teeth
will be false to you.
—*Dental proverb*

Psychiatrist to his nurse: "Just say we're very busy. Don't keep saying 'It's a madhouse.'"
—*Anonymous*

And then there was the psychiatrist who showed very poor taste when he equipped his waiting room with a cuckoo clock.
—*Ron Dentinger*

A psychiatrist and a proctologist hired a suite of offices for themselves and put up a sign, THE DEPARTMENT OF ODDS AND ENDS.
—*Isaac Asimov*

Hello, welcome to the Psychiatric Hotline:

If you are obsessive-compulsive, please press 1 repeatedly.

If you are codependent, please ask someone to press 2.

If you have multiple personalities, please press 3, 4, 5, and 6.

If you are paranoid-delusional, we know who you are and what you want. Just stay on the line so we can trace the call.

If you are schizophrenic, listen carefully and a little voice will tell you which number to press.

If you are manic-depressive, it doesn't matter which number you press. No one will answer.

—Jacquelyn Mayerhofer

Two successful psychoanalysts occupied an office in the same building. One was forty years old, the other was over seventy. They rode on the elevator together at the end of a hot, sticky day. The younger man was completely done in, and he noted with surprise that his senior was fresh as a daisy.

"I don't understand," he marveled, "how you can listen to patients from nine to five on a day like this and still look so cheerful when it's over."

The older analyst said simply, "Who listens?"

—*Anonymous*

My first psychiatrist said I was paranoid,
but I want to get a second opinion
because I think he's out to get me.
—*Tom Wilson ("Ziggy")*

After twelve years of therapy my psychiatrist
said something that brought tears
to my eyes. He said, *"No hablo inglès."*
—*Ronnie Shakes*

I told my psychiatrist I have suicidal
tendencies. He told me from now on
I have to pay in advance.
—*Rodney Dangerfield*

Secretary to Psychiatrist: Doctor, there is a patient here who thinks he is invisible.

Psychiatrist: Tell him I can't see him right now.

—*Anonymous*

Psychiatrist: This is your first visit, so I need to know a little bit about you. Tell me about yourself, starting at the beginning.

Patient: In the beginning, I created Heaven and Earth. . . .

—*Ron Dentinger*

Therapist: Do you smoke after sex?

Client: I don't know, I never checked.

—*Anonymous*

Psychiatry is the care of the id by the odd.
—*Anonymous*

A neurotic is the man who builds a castle in the air. A psychotic is the man who lives in it. And a psychiatrist is the man who collects the rents.
—*Lord Robert Webb-Johnstone*

I was once thrown out of a mental hospital for depressing the other patients.
—*Oscar Levant*

When we talk to God, we're praying. When God talks to us, we're schizophrenic.
—*Lily Tomlin*

Schizophrenia beats dining alone.
—*Oscar Levant*

Patient: Doctor, I have a split personality.

Psychiatrist: Nurse, bring in another chair.
—*Anonymous*

We need a twelve-step group for compulsive talkers. They could call it On Anon Anon.
—*Paula Poundstone*

I joined Liars Anonymous, but I had a lot of trouble finding them because they put the wrong address in all their ads.
—*J.J. Waugh*

Lotta self-help tapes out there. Got one called *How To Handle Disappointment.* I got it home and the box was empty.
—*Jonathan Droll*

I was forced to go to a positive thinking seminar. I couldn't stand it. So I went outside to the parking lot and let half the air out of everybody's tires. As they came out I said, "So, are your tires half full or half empty?"
—*Scott Derrickson*

My friend thought he was not gonna make it. Then he started thinking positive. Now he's positive he's not gonna make it.
—*Sammy Shore*

The problem with self-improvement is knowing when to quit.
—*David Lee Roth*

You've got to wonder if anyone proofreads those ads on television. Last night I saw this laxative ad where the main selling point was that the stuff works while you sleep. That doesn't sound too wonderful to me.

—*Ron Dentinger*

Have you seen the new home surgery kit available via order? It's called Suture Self.

—*Anonymous*

Did you know if you laid every cigarette smoker end-to-end around the world more than 67 percent of them would drown?
—*Steve Altman*

You wanna see drug-related violence— ban cigarettes in the United States.
—*Marsha Doble*

It is now proved beyond doubt that smoking is one of the leading causes of statistics.
—*Fletcher Knebel*

"Ladies, gentlemen, and extinguished guests . . ."

I have every sympathy with the American who was so horrified by what he had read of the effects of smoking that he gave up reading.
—*Henry G. Strauss*

Those nicotine patches seem to work pretty well, but I understand it's pretty hard to keep 'em lit.
—*George Carlin*

To cease smoking is the easiest thing I ever did. I ought to know because I've done it a thousand times.
—*Mark Twain*

A woman walked up to a little old man in a rocking chair on his porch. "I couldn't help noticing how happy you look," she said. "What's your secret for a long, happy life?"

"I smoke three packs of cigarettes a day," he said. "I also drink a case of whiskey a week, eat fatty foods, and never exercise."

"That's amazing," the woman said. "How old are you?"

"Twenty-six," he said.

—Joe Claro

If you resolve to give up smoking, drinking, and loving, you don't actually live longer; it just seems longer.

—Clement Freud

I read this article. It said the typical symptoms of stress are eating too much, smoking too much, impulse buying, and driving too fast. Are they kidding? This is my idea of a great day!
—*Monica Piper*

I know a man who gave up smoking, drinking, sex, and rich food. He was healthy right up to the time he killed himself.
—*Johnny Carson*

When I was young, I kissed my first woman and smoked my first cigarette on the same day. Believe me, never since have I wasted any more time on tobacco.
—*Arturo Toscanini*

Health—what my friends are always
drinking to before they fall down.
—*Phyllis Diller*

The man who enters a bar very
optimistically often comes out
very misty optically.
—*Leopold Fechtner*

My grandmother is over eighty and still doesn't need glasses. Drinks right out of the bottle.
—*Henny Youngman*

I'd hate to be an alcoholic with Alzheimer's. Imagine needing a drink and forgetting where you put it.
—*George Carlin*

I think tobacco and alcohol warnings are too general. They should be more to the point: "Warning! Alcohol will turn you into the same asshole your father was."
—*George Carlin*

Once, during Prohibition, I was forced to
live on nothing but food and water.
—W.C. Fields

I drink too much. Last time I gave a urine
sample there was an olive in it.
—Rodney Dangerfield

Only Irish coffee provides in a single glass all
four essential food groups: alcohol, caffeine,
sugar, and fat.
—Alex Levine

"You're getting pretty big yourself!"

I won't tell you how much I weigh, but don't get on the elevator with me unless you're going down.
—*Jack E. Leonard*

Let me put it this way. According to my girth, I should be a ninety-foot redwood.
—*Erma Bombeck*

I hate skinny women, especially when they say things like, "Sometimes I forget to eat." Now, I've forgotten my mother's maiden name . . . I've forgotten my car keys . . . but you've got to be a special kind of stupid to forget to eat.
—*Marsha Warfield*

I have flabby thighs, but fortunately,
my stomach covers them.
—*Joan Rivers*

Why am I bothering to eat this chocolate?
I might as well just apply it directly
to my thighs.
—*Rhoda Morgenstern*

I never worry about diets. The only carrots
that interest me are the kind you get
in a diamond.
—*Mae West*

Inside me there's a thin person struggling to get out, but I can usually sedate him with four or five cupcakes.
—*Bob Thaves*

Never eat more than you can lift.
—*Miss Piggy*

Every day I eat from the four basic food groups: milk chocolate, dark chocolate, white chocolate, and cocoa.
—*Debra Tracy*

I went on a diet. Had to go on two diets at the same time 'cause one diet wasn't giving me enough food.
—*Barry Marter*

I told my doctor I get very tired when I go on a diet, so he gave me pep pills. Know what happened? I ate faster.
—*Joe E. Lewis*

I've been dieting for a week, and all I've lost is seven days.
—*Pat Partridge*

Have you noticed when you go on a diet,
the first thing you lose is your temper.
—*Anonymous*

My wife went to one of those diet doctors
and in two months, she lost $300.
—*Anonymous*

No diet will remove all the fat from your body
because the brain is entirely fat.
Without a brain you may look good, but
all you could do is run for public office.
—*Covert Bailey*

I asked the kid what he'll do when he's
big like me. He said, "Diet."
—*Ron Dentinger*

I have a great diet—you're allowed to eat
anything you want, but you must eat it with
naked fat people.
—*Ed Bluestone*

I found there was only one way to look thin—
hang out with fat people.
—*Rodney Dangerfield*

"I'll give you five bucks if you'll put eight miles on this thing before your father gets home."

Fat people don't think like thin people. Did you ever go up to a fat person on the street and ask them where something is? They tell you—like this is where the difference really shows—"Well, go down there to Arby's. Go right past Wendy's, McDonalds, Burger King, Taco Bell, Kentucky Fried Chicken. It's the chocolate brown building."

—*Roseanne*

**Exercise equipment for sale.
Fat guy wants money for sofa.**
—*Ad from the Sonora Union-Democrat, Oct. 29, 1990*

If you cheat on a diet you gain in the end.
—*Leopold Fechtner*

Always use one of the new—and far more
reliable—elastic measuring tapes
to measure your waistline.
—*Miss Piggy*

The waist is a terrible thing to mind.
—*Tom Wilson ("Ziggy")*

No matter what kind of diet you are on,
you can usually eat as much as you want
of anything you don't like.
—*Walter Slezak*

Nothing in the world arouses more false hopes
than the first four hours of a diet.
—*Anonymous*

You'll be hungry again in an hour.
—*Fortune cookie opened by Ziggy (Tom Wilson)*

The toughest part of a diet isn't watching what you eat. It's watching what other people eat.
—*Jeff Rovin*

The only way to keep your health is to eat what you don't want, drink what you don't like, and do things you'd rather not.
—*Mark Twain*

Most diets can be summed up with this advice: If it tastes good, spit it out.
—*Fred Metcalf*

We sneak another midnight snack
And think no one will know it;
But those who don't count calories
Have figures that will show it.

—*Charles Ghigna*

It is of no concern to me how many calories there are in *one* chocolate chip cookie. What I need to know is: How many calories are there in a *batch* of chocolate chip cookies? And, are there fewer in the dough?
—*Susan Vass*

In two decades I've lost a total of 789 pounds. I should be hanging from a charm bracelet.
—*Erma Bombeck*

I have gained and lost the same ten pounds so many times over that my cellulite must have déjà vu.
—*Jane Wagner*

"We've got to stop taking our vitamins before dinner. I'm full."

Did you ever see the customers in health-food stores? They are pale, skinny people who look half dead. In a steak house, you see robust, ruddy people. They're dying, of course, but they look terrific.
—*Bill Cosby*

Old people shouldn't eat health food. They need all the preservatives they can get.
—*Anonymous*

I did not rise to the top of the food chain to become a vegetarian.
—*Bumper sticker*

I am pushing sixty—
that's enough exercise for me.
—*Mark Twain*

My grandmother started walking five miles a day when she was sixty. She's ninety-seven now and we don't now where the hell she is.
—*Ellen DeGeneres*

I like long walks, especially when they are taken by people who annoy me.
—*Fred Allen*

The advantage of exercising everyday
is that you die healthier.
—*Anonymous*

I'm not into working out. My philosophy:
No pain, no pain.
—*Carol Leifer*

If you are going to try cross-country skiing,
start with a small country.
—*From Saturday Night Live*

I have to exercise in the morning before my brain figures out what I'm doing.
—*Marsha Doble*

And now for your morning exercise. Ready? Up, down, up, down, up, down, up, down. And now the other eyelid.
—*Fred Metcalf*

I don't exercise at all. If God had meant us to touch our toes, He would have put them farther up on our body.
—*Gene Perret*

The only reason I would take up jogging is so that I could hear heavy breathing again.
—*Erma Bombeck*

My doctor recently told me that jogging could add years to my life. He was right. I feel ten years older already.
—*Milton Berle*

I don't jog. It makes the ice jump right out of my glass.
—*Martin Mull*

I joined a health club last year, spent about 400 bucks. Haven't lost a pound. Apparently you have to show up.
—*Rich Ceisler*

I try to spend an hour at the club every day now. That includes a ten-minute whirlpool, ten-minute sauna, and forty minutes circling the parking lot looking for a space near the door.
—*Susan Vass*

I'm not saying all aerobics instructors are dumb. I'm simply saying I have doubts about my aerobics instructor due to the fact that she is constantly warning us,
"Don't forget to breathe."
—*Susan Vass*

"You'll probably find this considerably more strenuous than other treadmill tests you've taken."

SOME SIGNS THAT OLD AGE MIGHT BE
CREEPING UP ON YOU:

When you like to be in crowds because they keep
you from falling down.

When your only party of the last year was to
celebrate the twelfth rerun of your seven-year
itch.

When the parts that have arthritis are the
parts where you feel the best.

When your favorite section of the newspaper is
"25 Years Ago Today."

When your sex drive shifts from cruise control
to neutral.

When a big evening with your friends is sitting
around comparing living wills.

When your knees buckle but your belt won't.

When your clothes go into the overnight bag so you can fill the suitcase with your pills.

When you resent the annual swimsuit issue of *Sports Illustrated* because there are fewer articles to read.

When your idea of a change of scenery is looking to the left or right.

When somebody you consider an old-timer calls you an old-timer.

When you find you're no longer worried about being involved in a paternity suit.

—*George Burns*

Getting old has its advantages. I can no longer read the bathroom scale.
—Brad Schreiber

I'm at an age when my back goes out more than I do.
—Phyllis Diller

The secret of longevity is to keep breathing.
—Bruce Lansky

ON THE VANITY OF EARTHLY GREATNESS

The tusks that clashed in mighty brawls
Of mastodons, are billiard balls.

The sword of Charlemagne the Just
Is ferric oxide, known as rust.

The grizzly bear whose potent hug
Was feared by all, is now a rug.

Great Caesar's bust is on the shelf,
And I don't feel so well myself.
                    —*Arthur Guiterman*

I prefer old age to the alternative.
—*Maurice Chevalier*

Either this man is dead or
my watch has stopped.
—*Groucho Marx*

There are many ways to die in bed,
but the best is not alone.
—*George Burns*

Two old guys wonder if there's baseball in heaven, and promise each other that the first to die will somehow let the other one know. A week later, one of them dies. And a week after that, his friend recognizes his voice coming down from the clouds. "Joe, I've got some good news and some bad news," the disembodied voice reports. "The good news is that there *is* a baseball team in heaven. The bad news is that you're pitching on Friday."

—*Anonymous*

A wealthy man lay critically ill. "There's only one thing that will save you," his doctor said. "A brain transplant. It's experimental and very expensive."

"Money is no object," the man said. "Can you get a brain?"

"There are three available. The first was from a college professor, but it'll cost you $10,000."

"Don't worry, I can pay. What about the second?"

"It was from a rocket scientist. It'll cost you $100,000."

"I have the money. And I'd be a lot smarter, too. But what about the third?"

"The third came from a Washington bureaucrat. It will set you back half a million dollars."

"Why so much for the bureaucrat's brain?" the patient asked.

"Never been used."

—Anonymous

MEDICAL EXAMINER'S FINDINGS:

1. The patient didn't die of anything serious.

2. The man had never been fatally ill before.

3. Cause of death is unknown as patient died without the aid of a doctor.

4. Went to bed feeling on top of the world but when he woke up he was dead.

5. The cause of death was an act of God under very suspicious circumstances.

6. The patient died in a state of perfect health.

7. Suspected suicide, though the patient later denied this.

—*Des MacHale*

CELEBRITY EPITAPHS:

Dorothy Parker: Excuse my dust.

Jack Benny: Did you hear about my operation?

Robert Benchley: All of this is over my head.

Leo Rosten: This is much too deep for me.
—*Anonymous*

The death rate is the same everywhere—
100 percent—if you wait long enough.
—*Leo Rosten*

103

INDEX

Order Form

Qty.	Title	Author	Order #	Unit Cost (U.S. $)	Total
	Age Happens	Lansky, B.	4025	$7.00	
	Are You Over the Hill?	Dodds, B.	4265	$7.00	
	Dads Say the Dumbest Things	Lansky/Jones	4220	$7.00	
	Familiarity Breeds Children	Lansky, B.	4015	$7.00	
	For Better And For Worse	Lansky, B.	4000	$7.00	
	Golf: It's Just a Game!	Lansky, B.	4035	$7.00	
	Grandma Knows Best	McBride, M.	4009	$7.00	
	How to Line Up Your Fourth Putt	Rusher, B.	4075	$7.00	
	How to Survive Your 40th Birthday	Dodds, B.	4260	$7.00	
	Laugh Twice and Call Me in the Morning	Lansky, B.	4065	$7.00	
	Moms Say the Funniest Things	Lansky, B.	4280	$7.00	
	What's So Funny about Getting Old	Fischer/Noland	4205	$7.00	
	Work and Other Occupational Hazards	Lansky, B.	4016	$7.00	
	You're No Spring Chicken	Fischer, E.	4215	$7.00	
				Subtotal	
			Shipping and Handling (see below)		
			MN residents add 6.5% sales tax		
				Total	

YES! Please send me the books indicated above. Add $2.00 shipping and handling for the first book with a retail price up to $9.99, or $3.00 for the first book with a retail price over $9.99. Add $1.00 shipping and handling for each additional book. All orders must be prepaid. Most orders are shipped within two days by U.S. Mail (7–9 delivery days). Rush shipping is available for an extra charge. Overseas postage will be billed.
Quantity discounts available upon request.

Send book(s) to:

Name_____ Address _____

City_____ State ___ Zip _____ Telephone (____) _____

Payment via:

❑ Check or money order payable to Meadowbrook Press

❑ Visa (for orders over $10.00 only) ❑ MasterCard (for orders over $10.00 only)

Account # _____ Signature _____ Exp. Date _____

You can also phone or fax us with a credit card order.

A *FREE* Meadowbrook Press catalog is available upon request.

Mail to: Meadowbrook Press, 5451 Smetana Drive, Minnetonka, MN 55343

Phone (612) 930-1100   Toll-Free 1-800-338-2232   Fax (612) 930-1940

For more information (and fun) visit our website: www.meadowbrookpress.com